Profiles in American History

The Life and Times of

WILLIAM PENN

Mitchell Lane PUBLISHERS

P.O. Box 196 · Hockessin, Delaware 19707

Profiles in American History

Titles in the Series

The Life and Times of

Alexander Hamilton
Benjamin Franklin
Betsy Ross
Eli Whitney
George Rogers Clark
Hernando Cortés
John Adams
John Cabot
John Hancock
John Peter Zenger
Nathan Hale
Patrick Henry
Paul Revere
Samuel Adams
Sir Walter Raleigh
Susan B. Anthony
Thomas Jefferson
William Penn

Profiles in American History

The Life and Times of

WILLIAM PENN

Bonnie Hinman

Mitchell Lane
PUBLISHERS

Printed and bound in the United States of America.

Printing 1 2 3 4 5 6 7 8 9

Library of Congress Cataloging-in-Publication Data
Hinman, Bonnie.
The life and times of William Penn / by Bonnie Hinman.
p. cm. — (Profiles in American history)
Includes bibliographical references and index.
ISBN 1-58415-433-0 (library bound : alk. paper)
1. Penn, William, 1644–1718—Juvenile literature. 2. Pioneers—Pennsylvania—Biography—Juvenile literature. 3. Quakers—Pennsylvania—Biography—Juvenile literature. 4. Pennsylvania—History—Colonial period, ca. 1600–1755—Juvenile literature I. Title. II. Series.
F152.2.H56 2006
974.8'02092—dc22 2005028491

ISBN-10: 1-58415-433-0 ISBN-13: 978-1-58415-433-4

ABOUT THE AUTHOR: Bonnie Hinman, a writer for over thirty years, particularly enjoys writing about the colonial period in our country's history. William Penn played a big role in the founding of America, and Bonnie loved learning more about him. Bonnie graduated from Missouri State University and has taught creative writing at Crowder College. Her books for Mitchell Lane Publishers include *Florence Nightingale and the Advancement of Nursing* and *Pennsylvania: William Penn and the City of Brotherly Love*. Her book *A Stranger in His Own House: The Story of W.E.B. Du Bois* (Morgan Reynolds) was chosen for the 2006 New York Public Library's Books for the Teen Age. She lives in Joplin, Missouri, with her husband, Bill, two cats, and three dogs.

PHOTO CREDITS: Cover, pp. 1, 3—Stock Montage/Getty Images; p, 6—Hulton Archive/Getty Images; p. 8—Time Life Pictures/Getty Images; p. 12—Archive Photos/Getty Images; p. 14—Musée du Louvre; p. 17—Sharon Beck; pp. 18, 23, 25, 28, 33, 34—Library of Congress; p. 20—National Maritime Museum; p. 36—Explore PA History.

PUBLISHER'S NOTE: This story is based on the author's extensive research, which she believes to be accurate. Documentation of such research is contained on page 46.

The internet sites referenced herein were active as of the publication date. Due to the fleeting nature of some web sites, we cannot guarantee they will all be active when you are reading this book.

PLB

Contents

Chapter One
The New Colony 7
*FYInfo: The Lenni Lenape 11
Chapter Two
The Sea Captain's Son 13
FYInfo: Oliver Cromwell 19
Chapter Three
The Inner Light 21
FYInfo: The Great Plague of London 27
Chapter Four
The Holy Experiment 29
FYInfo: George Fox 35
Chapter Five
Years of Struggle 37
FYI: Pennsbury Manor 42
Chapter Notes 43
Chronology 44
Timeline in History 45
Further Reading 46
For Young Adults 46
Works Consulted 46
On the Internet 46
Glossary 47
Index 48
*For Your Information

Many paintings were done showing William Penn standing near the famous "Treaty Elm." There was no official record of Penn's meeting with the Native Americans, but artists of that time painted their own versions of the legend.

CHAPTER 1

The New Colony

The green forested shoreline of Delaware Bay was a sight to cause rejoicing among the passengers of the *Welcome* in late October 1682. William Penn was one of the fortunate who survived the two-month journey from England on the small ship.

Two months was considered a fairly quick trip in that time. This voyage would have been a great success had it not been for the smallpox epidemic that broke out soon after the 100 or so travelers began their voyage. Since Penn had caught smallpox as a child, he was immune to the disease and was able to help care for the sick and dying passengers. One of the passengers later said of Penn in an account of the voyage, "His singular care was manifested in contributing to the necessities of many who were sick of the small-pox then on board, of which about 30 died."[1]

William Penn was the new proprietor of Pennsylvania, recently created, named, and given to Penn by King Charles II of England. Penn had great plans for this new land and must have been thrilled as he was escorted off the *Welcome* at New Castle on the Delaware River.

With great formality he was presented with the key to the fort there and with a piece of grassy sod implanted with a twig. Along with some water from the Delaware, this signified the transfer of property to Penn.

William Penn receives the charter of Pennsylvania from King Charles II in 1681. The land was given in payment for a debt that Charles II owed to Penn's father.

The residents of New Castle and the surrounding area warmly greeted Penn and pledged their allegiance to him. Settlers from several countries lived in this land between Maryland and New York, including Swedes and Dutch. Many Native Americans also waited to see this man who had sent them a friendly letter in advance of his arrival.

The travelers reboarded the *Welcome* and went up the Delaware River to Upland. There, legend says, Penn allowed a fellow passenger from the ship to rename the little town Chester in honor of the man's hometown in England.

During this time Penn sent goodwill messages to the two neighboring colonies and asked for an appointment to meet with Lord Baltimore of Maryland. Some boundary questions remained, and Penn hoped to settle them quickly.

Meanwhile Penn continued his trip up the Delaware by barge and by boat. The river's forested banks were bright with autumn color and thick with birds and deer and other creatures. This was a satisfying sight to Penn, who was devoting a great deal of his personal fortune to develop this wilderness into a welcoming new land for all people.

Soon the barge came in sight of high bluffs above the river. The Lenni Lenape called this place Coaquannock, meaning "Grove of Tall Pines." Penn had instructed his land commissioners to choose a high and dry spot for the site of the beautiful city he planned. It would be called Philadelphia, which in Greek means "city of brotherly love."

Some houses were already there, and the brick Blue Anchor Tavern had been there for at least ten years. Penn's barge nosed into a sandy beach at the base of the bluffs. He was greeted by the canoes of local American Indians and by the residents of the tiny town. He was pleased with what he saw as he toured the site of his future city. Streets and some house lots had been marked according to the plans Penn had sent. The streets were wide, and there were open spaces allowed for parks.

Penn's barge had at least one more stop to make as he continued up the Delaware River. Penn's deputy, William Markham, had just the previous summer purchased a parcel of land from the Native American sachems, or chiefs. It was where Penn's home would be built. Penn called it Pennsbury, and construction may have begun even before he arrived. The large estate was planned as a home for Penn and his wife and children when they could join him in Pennsylvania.

Penn turned immediately to taking care of the business of his colony. On November 2, he convened a court session at New Castle. He gave instructions about surveys, grants, and land titles and announced another court session to settle any disputes. He declared that until laws and regulations could be made for the new colony, Pennsylvania residents would be governed by the existing laws of the province of New York.

Sometime later in November, one of Penn's most famous meetings probably took place. There is no written record of his meeting with the Native Americans, but oral tradition makes it likely that it did take place soon after Penn's arrival in Pennsylvania.

At least three different Indian groups met with Penn and his council and assistants. The Delaware, also called the Lenni Lenape, the Mingoes, and the Shawnees met with Penn so that he could further assure them of his good intentions toward them. Again tradition says that the meeting took place just north of the site for Philadelphia at a place called Shackamaxon.

The location was reported to be near a huge old elm tree, which took the name Treaty Elm in stories passed down among both the Native Americans and the settlers. The Native Americans were dressed in their finest garb, and the event proceeded with much formality. The chiefs sat in a great circle with their warriors immediately behind them, and farther back the young men, women, and children sat or stood.

William Penn wore his traditional English clothing but added a wide blue sash around his waist to honor those he was meeting. The name Great Treaty, which was given to the conference, probably didn't recognize any particular agreement between Penn and the Native Americans. The Native Americans were known not to make any formal agreements about land purchases or any other transactions without a great deal of talk among themselves.

This fact makes it likely that this meeting was simply a friendship agreement during which William Penn promised to deal fairly with the Native Americans, and they offered honorable behavior in return. The Native Americans certainly remembered Penn's promises and retained great respect and admiration for the man they called Onas, meaning "the pen."

Later a French writer, Voltaire, made the Great Treaty more famous by saying that it was the only treaty between European settlers and the Native Americans that was never broken. Certainly Penn never broke his word.

The Lenni Lenape

Penn's Treaty with the Native Americans

The Lenni Lenape were called the Delaware by Europeans because their lands were near the Delaware River. The Lenape were one of the Native American tribes with which William Penn negotiated for purchase of their land.

The Lenape lived in small villages, which were usually near creeks or other water. The land around the Delaware River was a wilderness of forest and streams with good hunting. The Lenape hunted and fished and gathered wild plants, but in the spring and summer, they raised crops on small plots of land.

The Lenape had fought successfully against the Dutch and Swedish settlers who lived in the sparsely populated area around the Delaware. However, the diseases brought to them by the European settlers had greatly reduced their numbers. Near the time William Penn arrived, they had been defeated by another Native American tribe, the Iroquois. In spite of that defeat, the Iroquois didn't win the right to sell the Lenape lands.

The Lenape chiefs negotiated the sale of their tribal lands, but there were often overlapping rights. Sometimes that made it necessary for Penn to pay more than one chief for the same land. Penn understood this and dealt fairly with the Native Americans.

The Lenape and other area Native Americans came to greatly respect Penn and his fellow Quakers. This respect lingered for many years after Penn returned to England. In the middle of the eighteenth century, during a war in which some of the Native American tribes tried to win back their lands, Quaker settlers were largely spared the warfare.

The Lenape were gradually pushed west. First they went to Indiana and then to Missouri and Oklahoma. Eventually they no longer lived together as one tribe.

William Penn's father, also named William Penn, was an admiral in the British Navy. He sailed with the British fleet to the Mediterranean and to help fight a war with Holland. He commanded the fleet that sailed to the New World to conquer Spanish possessions there.

CHAPTER 2

The Sea Captain's Son

William Penn's father was a sea captain when his first child was born in October 1644. The father's name was William, too, and he had been lucky enough to be in port near London when his son was born. His ship, the *Fellowship,* didn't have to leave for its next assignment until after the tiny baby had been baptized at the nearby All Hallows Church.

The Penns lived on Tower Hill within sight of the Tower of London in a small but comfortable house. At age twenty-three, William Penn Sr. was quickly making a name for himself in the British Navy. It was an exciting time for an ambitious seaman. The middle of the seventeenth century was marked with civil war and unrest in Britain. King Charles I got in over his head as he tried to manipulate Parliament to run Britain's government the way he wanted.

At last Parliament rebelled, raised an army, and fought directly against the king's forces. During the civil wars that followed, Oliver Cromwell proved himself as a military commander. King Charles fought hard against the uprisings but refused to compromise when it became clear that most of the people didn't support him. He was tried and executed in January 1649.

King Charles I reigned in England from 1625 until he was executed for treason on January 30, 1649. He opposed Parliament in what became the English Civil War. He had been a sickly child and was rather short at five feet four inches tall.

For eleven years Britain was ruled as a commonwealth by a parliament or assembly. There was still much unrest, with little agreement about the form of government Britain should take. At last Cromwell was appointed Lord Protector, a title he preferred to that of king. King or not, Cromwell was in charge of Britain from December 1653 until his death from a bout of malaria in September 1658.

Penn Senior was a rising star in the British Navy. Although he captained ships that aided Parliament and Oliver Cromwell, Penn remained a loyalist to Charles I and to other Stuart family members. He worked for the government because it paid him on a fairly regular basis, but he wanted Charles II, who had been exiled, to reconcile with the other government leaders.

Son William was a small boy during these unsettled times in Britain. He lived with his mother in London while his father patrolled the Irish Sea and helped put down uprisings on the Irish coast and elsewhere. Penn Senior rose up the ladder of command and was named a general and then Rear Admiral of the Irish Seas.

Unrest continued and finally Admiral Penn could afford to move his family out of London to a country home in Wanstead. At that time London was a disease-ridden, brawling city.

There were other dangers in London as well. Oliver Cromwell was a Puritan and greatly disapproved of the Anglican Church, which had always been the official church in Britain. In fact it was called the Church of England. Puritans didn't like the rituals and requirements of the official church and especially the corruption they saw in the ministers of that church.

The political and religious storms that raged during William's childhood years didn't disturb his day-to-day life in Wanstead. William attended Chigwell School, which was about four miles from his home. Schooldays were long, as they began at six o'clock in the morning in summer and ended at six in the afternoon. In winter William had to be at school at seven and stay until five in the afternoon. He learned Latin and Greek as well as English grammar and spelling. William was a good student and enjoyed his days of school.

Admiral Penn came home for visits to his family, which now included a baby daughter, Margaret. William loved these visits as his father would enthusiastically tell the exciting stories of his time at sea. The admiral was highly thought of by Cromwell and his council. Cromwell awarded some land in Ireland to Penn in payment for losses of land that Mrs. Penn's family had suffered during the rebellion in Ireland many years before.

Toward the end of William's years at Chigwell School, he had what he later described as a visit from God. He was alone in his bedroom or perhaps a classroom when he felt a sudden inward peace with a brightening of the room. He thought that perhaps God was calling him to a holy life, although he didn't know then what form this life would take.

The quiet and comfortable years at Wanstead ended abruptly when William was eleven. Mrs. Penn, William, and baby Margaret were called to London because Admiral Penn had been arrested. Cromwell and his council accused the admiral of disobeying orders. Admiral Penn had been sent with an army general to take the island of Hispaniola in the Caribbean. The mission had gone wrong, and Hispaniola couldn't be taken, so the commanders had decided to take the island of Jamaica instead. Although Jamaica was a better prize than Hispaniola, Cromwell was angered and ordered the commanders arrested.

Penn spent five weeks imprisoned in the Tower of London. After much questioning he was released. Cromwell was not able to prove that Penn had deliberately disobeyed orders.

The elder Penn had always been an accomplished politician, able to read the currents that swirled around Cromwell and among the loyalists who wanted the return of a Stuart king. He judged that it was a good time for him to quit his job in the navy and leave London. On August 12, 1656, he loaded up his family and took them to Ireland.

The Penns took over the land that Cromwell had given them at Macroom in County Cork. Around this time a third child, Richard, was born to the Penns. Their new home was a large stone castle, which stood in the midst of a village of thatched cottages.

William Penn Sr. had more time to spend with William than ever before. He taught his son how to manage an estate, how to defend himself, and how to be a gentleman in manners and appearance.

When William was thirteen, a visitor came to Macroom Castle who was to influence the young man's life beyond imagining. The elder Penn, who was curious about the people called Quakers, invited a traveling Quaker preacher named Thomas Loe to speak at the castle.

Quakers, a religious group, believe that people do not need a priest or minister to talk to God for them, that God is ready to listen to each person directly. At their meetings, they often sit quietly together waiting for someone to feel led to stand up and speak. In Penn's time, the Quakers had been attracting attention in England and Ireland and other places as well.

The room was quiet before Loe rose to speak in Macroom Castle. He spoke eloquently of the "Inner Light" that was avail-

Haiti and the Dominican Republic make up the Caribbean island of Hispaniola. In Penn's time, they were Spanish territories, as was Jamaica. Penn's father, Admiral William Penn, was arrested after he and army General Robert Venables failed in their attempt to take Hispaniola for Britain but took Jamaica instead.

able to each man and woman. His listeners had likely never heard such ideas before and were deeply impressed. However, after speaking, Loe moved on to another town to teach, and Castle Macroom largely returned to normal. One exception, perhaps, was young William, who thought long and hard about what he had heard.

The Irish years passed peacefully enough, and eventually the time came to return to London. Cromwell had died and his son had lasted less than a year as Lord Protector. People were ready for a change from the military rule and uncertainty of Cromwell's time. There was an election, and Admiral Penn was elected to a new House of Commons. There was open talk of bringing back

The Tower of London is one of the British Royal Palaces and has served as a fortress, observatory, treasury, zoo, and prison. It was best known for housing royal prisoners, some of whom were later executed for treason. Today it holds, among other treasures, the crown jewels.

Charles II from exile in Europe to be the new king. It was an exciting time, particularly for loyalists like Admiral Penn who had managed to survive Cromwell without giving up allegiance to their king.

William's youth had passed and now he was swept back to London along with his family to celebrate a new day rid of the Puritans and full of joy over the restoration of the monarchy. The things William had learned from his father and the experiences he had while in Ireland would greatly influence his adult life.

Oliver Cromwell

Oliver Cromwell was born into a landed gentry family in 1599. He went to a free school and spent a year at Sidney Sussex College, where he was better known for his love of sports than for his academic abilities.

During his late twenties, Cromwell experienced a spiritual awakening, which led him to have deep and lasting Puritan beliefs. These beliefs guided his behavior for the rest of his life.

He was a Member of Parliament several different times and soon found himself on the opposite side of the reigning King Charles I. Cromwell was a radical Puritan who wanted to abolish the national church in England. He wanted people to make their own choices about religion.

When the English Civil Wars started, Cromwell became a soldier. In spite of his inexperience, he was exceedingly successful in his new job. This success eventually led Parliament to put him in charge of their army. Cromwell wanted to restore King Charles to the throne because a peaceful settlement would be better for Britain. King Charles I would not compromise and eventually was executed.

Cromwell was in charge, but he made it clear that he didn't want to be named king. He proposed that he be called Lord Protector, which was a title that went back to the fifteenth century in England. In spite of his title, Cromwell was increasingly treated like a king. When he was reinstalled in 1657, the ceremony looked a lot like a coronation, with purple velvet robes and a golden scepter.

Cromwell's health declined quickly near the end of his life. His death may have been hastened by his grief over the death of his favorite daughter, Elizabeth, of cancer the month before he died.

For Your Information

Samuel Pepys was an ambitious young man who became one of the most famous diary writers ever. The details of daily life in the upper class were recorded from January 1, 1660, until May 31, 1669, when his diaries ended. Penn's father, Sir William, was mentioned often in the diaries, and there are several references to Penn the son.

CHAPTER 3

The Inner Light

Admiral Penn traveled with the fleet of ships that sailed to Holland in May 1660 to escort home Charles II, who would take his father's place as king. The new king came on board the escort ship, and one of his first acts was to name Penn a knight, allowing him to be called Sir William Penn for the rest of his life. It was a great honor and probably indicates that Penn had done some secret service for the exiled king.

William, the son, was enrolled at Oxford and began classes in October 1660. He enjoyed his lessons and did well. The next spring he went back to London to attend the coronation of King Charles II. It was a lavish affair, with parades, parties, banquets, and theater visits. London was throwing off the sober years of Cromwell with a spectacular event.

William and his family watched the coronation parade from some rented rooms above the route. Friends of his father's, including the famous diary writer Samuel Pepys, also gathered to watch the procession pass below. In his diary, Pepys recorded, "So glorious was the show with gold and silver, that we were not able to look at it, our eyes at last being so much overcome."[1]

William returned to Oxford to his studies. The jubilant mood of the country soon turned darker. Persecution of Puritans and

Quakers resumed as Parliament once again made the Anglican Church the only recognized church in Britain.

Penn became friends with other students who refused to obey some of the school's rules about chapel attendance and proper dress. These students held their own worship services and attended lectures by a former professor at Oxford. He was a Puritan nonconformist who encouraged the young men in their refusal to obey the rules.

First the students were fined for their behavior, but that didn't stop them. In March 1662, William Penn was expelled from Oxford and sent home.

He was met by an angry and embarrassed Sir William. Penn later wrote "of being banished from college; the bitter usage I underwent when I returned to my father, whipping, beating and turning out of doors in 1662."[2] Sir William was disappointed that his plans for his son to become an important player at the king's court were not proceeding smoothly.

William's mother quickly rescued him from the street, and Sir William cooled down enough to let the young man return to his home. Soon Sir William developed another plan to save his son from himself. Penn would undertake a trip to France and other European countries to complete his gentleman's education.

Penn left for Paris in July 1662. He spent time in Paris and traveled throughout France. He entered into the elaborate society that existed around the court of King Louis XIV.

Penn also spent a year and a half at a well-known school in Saumur on the Loire River. The headmaster, Moïse Amyraut, was famous for speaking and writing on behalf of religious liberty and toleration. The time Penn spent studying at this school would influence his thinking for all his life.

At last Sir William wrote his son to come home. William arrived in London in August 1664. His polished appearance must have pleased his father very much. Outwardly at least, the trip to the Continent had accomplished all that Sir William had desired.

In February 1665, Penn began studying law at Lincoln's Inn. His legal education was almost immediately interrupted when Sir William asked him to come along on his ship when the fleet

The gateway to Lincoln's Inn was through an arch between two square gatehouses. Lincoln's Inn was a school for legal training and usually served the sons of the wealthy like William Penn. It was one of four such schools in London at the time.

sailed out to war with Holland. Sir William and the king's brother, the Duke of York, were in charge of the fleet. Penn spent several weeks on the *Royal Charles* watching his father command an entire squadron.

At last Sir William sent his son home with messages for King Charles. This may have been the father's way of introducing his son in a positive way. The king was cordial and attentive to the messenger who brought news from the fleet.

Finally Penn was back at school at Lincoln's Inn, but not for long. The school closed in June when an epidemic of bubonic plague overtook London. Thousands died as the plague spread throughout the city. Most wealthy families fled to the country that dreadful summer. Quakers went house to house helping the plague victims and their survivors. The arrests and mistreatment of Quakers continued even as they died of the plague themselves after helping others.

Eventually the plague finished its work, and Penn returned to Lincoln's Inn. Sir William came home triumphantly from war but was suffering from a severe attack of gout. His health had begun to fail, and it was time to pass on some of his duties to his son and heir.

Father and son decided that William would go to Ireland to tend to matters there concerning their properties. Sir William's land at Macroom had been returned to its original owners after Charles II became king, but the king had given other Irish lands to the Penn family in its place.

Penn proved to be a capable manager of his father's estates in Ireland. During a brief uprising at a nearby garrison of soldiers, he also was found to have an aptitude for soldiering when he helped bring order back to the fortress at Carrickfergus. He thought that he might be cut out to be an army officer, but his father discouraged him. Sir William had much finer things in mind for his eldest son than a soldier's career.

Within a few months, Penn had estate business under control and returned to London for a visit and to attend his sister's wedding. After the wedding, he went back to Ireland and settled in at Shanagarry Castle. Soon after his return, he discovered that Thomas Loe, who had come to Macroom Castle to speak when Penn was a teenager, would be speaking at nearby Cork. Penn asked permission to attend.

The meeting was probably held in a private home. By this time Quakers were also called Friends. After silent prayer, a speaker rose to talk. The next one to rise was Thomas Loe.

It has been recorded that these were his opening words: "There is a faith that overcometh the world, and a faith that is overcome by the world."[3]

William Penn found that Loe seemed to speak directly to his searching heart. All of his previous religious experiences and life events had brought him to this evening. By the time the meeting was over, Penn knew that this would not be the only Friends meeting that he would attend.

The Fortress of Carrickfergus guarded a harbor in Ireland known now as Belfast Lough. The garrison there mutinied in 1666, and young William Penn proved to be an able soldier as he fought with the Earl of Arran to restore order. His skill with sword and musket brought him much praise from his superiors.

Soon he was regularly going to meetings and found himself drawn more and more to the inner light that Quakers said was from God and was available to all who seek it. Quakers were being daily persecuted in Ireland, and eventually Penn managed to be in the wrong place and was arrested. He was imprisoned briefly in Cork, and while there he wrote his first literary effort on behalf of the Friends. The letter he wrote obtained his release in short order, but word soon reached Sir William in London that his son had been arrested.

Sir William wrote several letters urging and then ordering his son home. Young Penn knew that it wouldn't be a pleasant visit, so he delayed obeying as long as he dared. At last he had to return home.

Sir William was almost beside himself at this turn of events. His eldest son was being trained for an important position in government. This Quaker business would not do at all. He was particularly upset about the Quakers' refusal to bow or raise their hats for anyone, even the king. He also didn't like that they referred to others by using *thee* and *thou* rather than the word *you*. Sir William saw both of these practices as disrespectful to men and women of rank.

Father and son couldn't agree on a compromise, so an uneasy truce reigned in the household. William sought out Friends meetings in London and once more became deeply involved in their lives and troubles. As could be expected, he was arrested once more. The magistrate recognized Penn, and instead of sending him to jail, sent a note to his father.

Sir William was under many pressures himself and this was the last straw with his stubborn son. He ordered him home. If his son planned to continue his Quaker practices, Sir William would turn him out of the house to fend for himself.

William did intend to continue and was quickly absorbed into the Quaker movement. His fellow Quakers provided housing and food for him. Penn began to write letters and tracts defending the faith. He also used the political connections he had to go to the court of King Charles and talk to the king's ministers on behalf of the persecuted Quakers.

He was arrested again after he published a tract called *The Sandy Foundation Shaken*. Authorities decided that Penn questioned the very nature of God in his writing. They could not tolerate such heresy, and Penn was imprisoned in the Tower of London for almost nine months. He was released only after he wrote another tract in which he explained his views more clearly.

Father and son reconciled, and Sir William was able to convince his son to return to Ireland to manage the estates once more. Penn obliged his ailing father. Soon, however, he was immersed once again in Quaker meetings and events in Ireland. He had more stature now. He was a strong speaker and powerful author, and he had gone to the Tower for the faith. He had found his purpose in life and pursued it wholeheartedly.

The Great Plague of London

Bubonic plague was also called the Black Death because victims developed black patches on their skin. This horrible disease was caused by a bacteria spread by infected fleas that lived on rats. Epidemics of the plague had occurred since ancient times in England, Europe, and China.

Cases of the disease were always present in crowded poor sections of London, but in the spring of 1665 the number of deaths rose alarmingly. By summer it was a full-blown epidemic. It spread throughout London and to surrounding areas.

A person usually caught the plague when he or she was bitten by an infected flea. It could be spread person to person by droplets sneezed or coughed from a sufferer onto someone else, but that wasn't the main way it spread. People tried all sorts of remedies to protect themselves, and the government enforced strict quarantine rules. Because no one knew what caused the plague, the remedies and quarantines weren't effective.

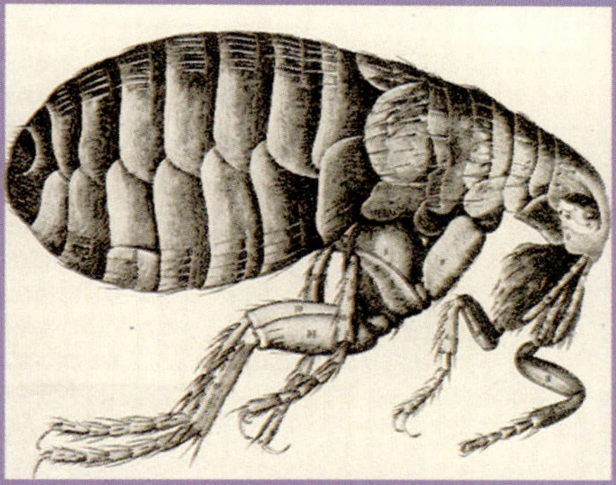
Close-up of a flea

Thousands of wealthy Londoners fled into the country to escape the plague, while thousands more lived on boats on the Thames River. The poor were hit the hardest. Authorities often boarded up victims' homes with family members in them. If they were lucky, someone would bring them food. Often the whole family died.

Records of deaths weren't reliable, but as many as 100,000 people may have died before colder weather in the fall killed the fleas. One legacy of the Great Plague that still exists is a nursery rhyme. In England it was sung this way:

Ring a ring o' roses
A pocketful of posies.
Atishoo! Atishoo!
We all fall down.

The rosy ring was a red rash that developed on victims, while the posies were small bouquets of flowers carried and sniffed because they were thought to prevent infection. *Atishoo* is the sneezing of the victim, and "we all fall down" means "we all die."

William Penn sailed back to England on the Endeavour, *above, after his first trip to Pennsylvania. The* Endeavour *had brought settlers and supplies to the new colony before returning to England with Penn. Penn landed in Sussex on October 6, 1684. The landing was within seven miles of his home, Worminghurst.*

CHAPTER 4

The Holy Experiment

Penn spent less than a year in Ireland and returned to England in early August 1670. He had barely arrived home before he was in trouble again. He was arrested for public preaching at Gracechurch Street Meeting House.

This arrest led Penn to make a significant contribution to the legal system in England. At his trial he used his speaking ability to persuade the jury that any charges of insurrection were false. The judge gave the jury instructions which left no doubt that the jurors were expected to find Penn guilty. It didn't matter whether or not they thought he committed any crime.

The jury came back with what amounted to a not-guilty verdict. They said he was guilty of speaking in Gracechurch Street but refused to say that he was guilty of unlawful assembly.

This verdict put the court in an uproar, and the judge declared that unless the jury found the defendant guilty as he had instructed them, he would put the whole lot of them in jail, too. They refused to change their minds and to pay the fines the court assessed. So they were carted off to Newgate Prison along with William Penn.

The case against the jurymen took some time to be resolved, but finally the highest court in England declared that a jury could not be punished for its verdict. This became legal precedent in

Britain and was the lasting legacy of William Penn and the jury that tried to vote their consciences.

Meanwhile Sir William was ill and quickly paid his son's fine so that he could come home. The loving and ambitious father did one more thing for his son. He wrote to the king and his brother, the Duke of York, and asked them to look kindly on his son. Both men sent their promises to the dying Sir William.

Sir William died on September 16, 1670. His son inherited most of his estates and money. He sincerely mourned the loss of his father. In spite of their differences, the pair had loved each other deeply.

Penn soon returned to traveling and writing to spread the Quaker religion. However, he had met and now courted Gulielma Springett. Guli was everything a devout Quaker could hope for in a wife. She was even tempered, modest, and beautiful. The couple married in the spring of 1672.

The next years were busy ones for the couple, and not without sadness. Their first three children died in infancy. It was a perilous time for babies, with many illnesses that could afflict them and very few effective treatments. Finally a sturdy boy, Springett, was born in 1675, and he survived. Eventually a sister, Letitia, and brother, William, were born and lived, too.

William did much writing during these years but stayed close to home. He helped the Quaker cause by publishing tracts and taking care of legal and administrative problems. George Fox, the founder of Quakerism, returned to England from traveling in the American colonies. He found Penn to be a huge help in tackling the mountain of letters and other correspondence that had to be written on behalf of the Friends.

Persecution had increased in Britain, and civil liberties were few. George Fox was arrested and Penn worked with others in London to get him fairly tried and freed.

Penn had heard stories about life in the American colonies for many years. Quakers already lived there, and many of Penn's friends had traveled to the colonies. They brought back stories of a green and fertile land. Penn wondered if a new life for Quakers might lie across the ocean in America.

He became more closely involved with the colonies when he was asked to arbitrate a dispute between two Quakers who owned land in West New Jersey. Penn used his legal experience and his experience managing his father's lands in Ireland to help him settle the dispute.

West New Jersey was a prospering place, but it was rather small. It couldn't possibly hold all the Quakers who might want to move there. But there was another large piece of land across the Delaware River from New Jersey, and it was just as desirable. This was the property Penn set his sights on for a safe haven for Quakers and any other people being persecuted.

Penn began the task of getting this land granted to him by the king and Parliament. In spite of the king's friendship with his father and kindness to Penn himself, the two didn't share many political views. There was no reason to think that King Charles would give land in America to a member of the Whig Party. Penn knew this and tried a different approach.

King Charles had owed a large sum of money to Penn's father. Loans to the king weren't unusual, and they were seldom paid back. Sir William wouldn't have expected repayment had he been alive. Nevertheless, Penn petitioned the king to give him land in America to pay off the debt owed to his father.

In spite of the existing debt, it was still a big surprise to most in England when King Charles agreed to the land grant. Some thought that it was the king's way of getting rid of a bunch of troublesome Quakers, who happened to be Whigs as well. Others wondered if this was the king's way of protecting the son of his longtime friend Sir William.

Whatever the reason, the land was officially granted to Penn on March 4, 1681. At the king's request, the colony was to be called Pennsylvania. *Sylvania* was Latin for "woods," and *Penn* referred to Sir William. The son preferred that the Penn name not be attached, as he thought it rather high-handed for a Quaker to name a property after himself, but the king insisted.

Penn began the work that precedes the actual settling of a new colony. To attract settlers, he advertised all over Britain and Ireland and the European continent. Prices and terms for land purchase and rental had to be determined. A government had to be planned and attempts made to be friendly to neighboring colonies. There were already settlers in Pennsylvania, and they had to be reassured that Penn meant for them to stay.

Penn wrote many letters to all these people, but the most famous one was to the Native Americans who lived in Pennsylvania. It began, "My friends: There is one great God and power that hath made the world and all things therein, to whom you, and I, and all people owe their being and well-being, and to whom you and I must one day give an account for all that we have done in the world."[1] He continued by assuring them that he held them in greatest respect and would always deal fairly with them. This letter he sent to the chiefs by way of commissioners who had gone ahead to Pennsylvania.

Penn called his new settlement a "Holy Experiment" for Quakers and other persecuted groups, but didn't emphasize this when advertising for investors and settlers. Rather he asked for many kinds of tradesmen and skilled craftsmen and simply offered them a free and just society in his new land.

Penn also planned the government for his colony. Called the Frame of Government, it was a model for free and fair authority. It included guidelines for the people to vote and change the Frame, which they would do over the next twenty years. The right of the people to change their own government was a rare privilege in the seventeenth century.

Penn also had to ready his personal life in England before he could travel to Pennsylvania. It was decided that Guli and the children would stay behind and join Penn later.

At last the plans were complete, and Penn could embark for Pennsylvania. There was a final flurry of letters of instruction for Guli and each of the children. The anguish he felt at leaving his family can be felt in his words. "My dear wife, remember thou wast the love of my youth, and much the joy of my life the most belov'd as well as most worthy of all my earthly comforts. . . . Now I am to leave without knowing whether I shall ever see thee more."[2] The *Welcome* set sail on the last day of August 1682.

After the ship landed and Penn traveled up the Delaware to see Philadelphia and Pennsbury and to meet the Native Americans

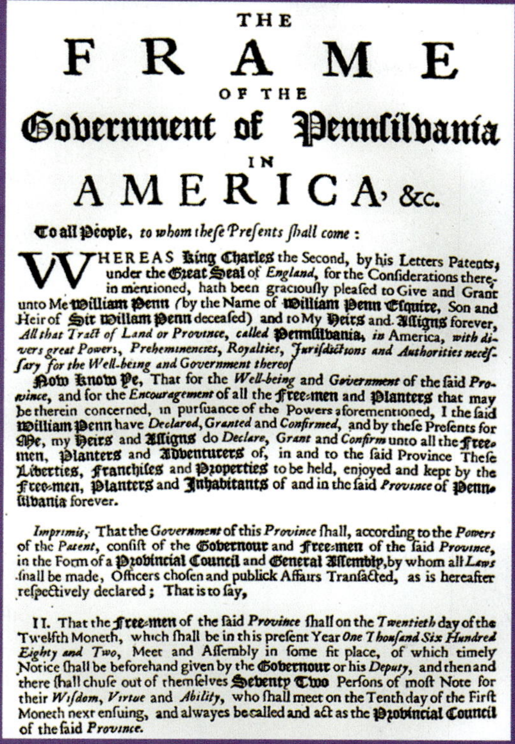

THE

FRAME

OF THE

Government of Pennſilvania

IN

AMERICA, &c.

To all People, *to whom theſe Preſents ſhall come* :

WHEREAS King Charles the Second, by his Letters Patents, under the Great Seal of *England*, for the Conſiderations therein mentioned, hath been graciouſly pleaſed to Give and Grant unto Me William Penn (by the Name of William Penn Eſquire, Son and Heir of Sir William Penn deceaſed) and to My Heirs and Aſſigns forever, *All that Tract of Land or Province, called* Pennſilvania, *in* America, *with divers great Powers, Preheminencies, Royalties, Juriſdictions and Authorities neceſſary for the Well-being and Government thereof*

Now know Ye, That for the *Well-being* and *Government* of the ſaid *Province*, and for the *Encouragement* of all the Free-men and Planters that may be therein concerned, in purſuance of the Powers aforementioned, I the ſaid William Penn have *Declared*, *Granted* and *Confirmed*, and by theſe Preſents for Me, my Heirs and Aſſigns do *Declare*, *Grant* and *Confirm* unto all the Free-men, Planters and Adventurers of, in and to the ſaid Province Theſe Liberties, Franchiſes and Properties to be held, enjoyed and kept by the Free-men, Planters and Inhabitants of and in the ſaid *Province* of Pennſilvania forever.

Imprimis, That the *Government* of this *Province* ſhall, according to the *Powers* of the *Patent*, conſiſt of the Governour and Free-men of the ſaid *Province*, in the Form of a Provincial Council and General Aſſembly, by whom all *Laws* ſhall be made, Officers choſen and publick Affairs Tranſacted, as is hereafter reſpectively declared; That is to ſay,

II. That the Free-men of the ſaid *Province* ſhall on the *Twentieth* day of the Twelfth Moneth, which ſhall be in this preſent Year *One Thouſand Six Hundred Eighty and Two*, Meet and Aſſembly in ſome fit place, of which timely Notice ſhall be beforehand given by the Governour or his *Deputy*, and then and there ſhall chuſe out of themſelves Seventy Two Perſons of moſt Note for their *Wiſdom*, *Virtue* and *Ability*, who ſhall meet on the Tenth day of the Firſt Moneth next enſuing, and alwayes be called and act as the Provincial Council of the ſaid *Province*.

The Frame of Government was the plan for governing Pennsylvania Colony. William Penn planned the government before he went to Pennsylvania in 1682. The Frame was revised several times, and each time more power was given to the people and their representatives.

who lived there, he settled in to work out the details of running his colony.

One of the more difficult tasks for Penn during this time was determining the boundary between Maryland and Pennsylvania. Lord Baltimore was not particularly helpful, and the dispute went on for years. The latitude lines had not been adequately placed, making the boundaries of the grants hard to determine. Penn tried his best to get Lord Baltimore to agree to a compromise, but it didn't happen.

Lots and tracts of land had to be assigned to settlers with all the resulting administrative tasks. During this time Penn often met with Native American leaders to reassure them of his continuing regard. He spoke of the Lenape language in a letter he wrote to investors in England in 1683: "I have made it my business to understand it that I might not want an interpreter on any occasion, and I must

When William Penn landed at New Castle in Pennsylvania Colony (now in Delaware) in 1682, he was greeted by settlers and Native Americans, including local officials. They were curious about their new governor.

say that I know not a language spoken in Europe that has words of more sweetness or greatness than theirs."[3]

The settlement of Pennsylvania went smoothly, but at last Penn decided that he would have to return to England to settle the boundary dispute with Lord Baltimore, who had already departed the colonies for home. Penn left detailed instructions for his steward at Pennsbury about the buildings and gardens.

Penn sailed for England on the *Endeavour* near the end of August 1684. He intended for his stay in England to be brief, after which he would bring Guli and the children back to Pennsylvania to live permanently in the new land he had come to love.

George Fox

George Fox, founder of the Quakers, was born in 1624 at Drayton-in-the-Clay in England. He was the son of a weaver, and although he had no formal education, he learned to read and write. His parents were members of the Church of England, and he showed an interest in religion at a young age.

He was apprenticed to a shoemaker, but at age nineteen he left home to wander the countryside in search of truth. It was a period of great confusion and torment for him. In time he began to formulate his own set of religious beliefs and teach them to others.

He believed that religious faith springs from an inner light that God gives to all who quietly seek him. He didn't believe that worship had to be in a church or be led by a minister. This was in direct conflict with the Church of England. Authorities weren't pleased to have someone traveling the countryside teaching beliefs and practices that went against the official church. Fox was arrested and jailed many times.

One of his appearances before a judge led to the name Quaker for the group of dissenters that Fox led. Up until then, Fox's followers were usually called Children of the Light. In Derby, England, one of the justices of the peace who had sentenced Fox to jail was warned by Fox to "tremble at the word of the Lord."[4] The judge laughed and scornfully called Fox and his companions Quakers. The label stuck, and over the years the name lost its negative meaning.

In 1653 Fox was arrested and taken to London to meet with the Lord Protector, Oliver Cromwell. The meeting went well as Fox explained Quaker beliefs and urged understanding and tolerance of Cromwell. It's likely that Fox had some measure of influence with Cromwell, because while the persecution didn't stop, it was alleviated.

Penn's second wife, Hannah Callowhill, was 20 years younger than her earnest suitor. He had known her family for many years before he started courting their shy daughter. Hannah was not easily convinced that the famous Quaker, William Penn, was the right husband for her—or rather, that she was the right wife for him.

CHAPTER
5

Years of Struggle

The voyage was fast, and soon Penn was reunited with his family. He discovered that King Charles was ill and had sent members of Parliament home. With a sick king and no Parliament in session, Penn realized that settling the dispute with Lord Baltimore was going to take much longer than he had expected.

Within a few months Charles II died, and his brother, the Duke of York, became King James II. James immediately had problems. He was a Catholic by faith, and the British people had always been afraid of him. They feared he would attempt to press his faith on his subjects as the official religion.

Penn and King James had long been friends, and Penn tried to advise the king. But James packed the Parliament with his supporters and allowed persecution of nonconformists to reach terrible levels of cruelty. It took delicate political maneuvering for William Penn to stay loyal to James yet express his dismay at some of the actions he took. Penn needed the king on his side to get the Pennsylvania boundaries straightened out.

Finally British leaders sent word to the king's eldest daughter, Mary, who lived in Holland, that they would support her if she would come back to England to take over the throne. She was married to William of Orange, who promptly set out to invade England and take the throne for his wife.

After much struggle James II fled to France and Mary returned. It was decided that she would rule together with her husband. Penn was left in the dangerous position of having supported the losing side.

He was arrested in 1689, accused of treason, but he was soon released when no evidence could be found to support the charge. During these years of political turmoil, Penn had to go into hiding. It was a difficult time of separation from his family with only occasional visits. Guli was in poor health, which made things harder for all of them.

At last Penn was cleared of suspicion and free to come and go. This good news was overshadowed by Guli's declining condition. Penn was by her side when she died on February 23, 1694. It took him a long time after Guli's death to recover his natural good spirits and energy.

Penn soon took up his travels again on behalf of Quakers. He resumed writing about the cause, publishing at least fourteen tracts, letters, and pamphlets in the years right after Guli's death.

He met a young woman on his travels who greatly interested him. Hannah Callowhill was twenty years younger than he, but there was something about the young Quaker woman that he admired. It took a long time to convince Hannah that she should marry him, but at last he was successful. His children liked her as well, so it was a happy day for the whole family when the couple married in March 1696.

A shadow lay over the event because Penn's elder son, Springett, was not well after having some kind of chest ailment. Springett's severe cough lingered, but all the family turned out for the wedding.

New bride Hannah returned to the Penn home to nurse Springett and then to comfort her husband when the young man died. Springett's death was a crushing blow to Penn. He had counted on his elder son to be a capable heir to Pennsylvania.

Penn worked steadily toward returning to Pennsylvania. Many issues arose to keep him in England, with finances at the top of the list. Landholders in Pennsylvania were not paying their quit-rents, and Penn's other holdings in Britain and Ireland were not producing the income they once had. Penn had entrusted much of his financial dealings to Philip Ford. This association had gone on for years because Penn trusted Ford. When Ford asked Penn to sign documents, Penn did so without hesitation.

At last most of the problems were resolved, allowing Penn, Hannah, and Letitia to leave for Pennsylvania on September 3, 1699. Son William had married and would remain in England. The voyage was long but uneventful, with the Penns reaching Pennsylvania on December 1.

Penn immediately plunged into the business of his colony. He wrote letters to the governors of surrounding colonies promising cooperation with them in solving any common problems. He met with the assembly and local Native American chiefs.

Penn was thrilled to see how Philadelphia had grown in his absence. There were many large and beautiful homes lining the wide streets. Trade was brisk along the dock, where ships unloaded their goods and reloaded with products from the city and countryside.

In January 1700, Hannah had a healthy boy, who was named John. He was Penn's only child born in America. When spring came, the whole Penn family traveled up the Delaware to Pennsbury. Hannah and Letitia took charge of the household, and soon visitors streamed to the graceful brick country home.

The family's happy time in Pennsylvania was ended by bad news from England. It looked as if England was going to war against France. If that happened, the English colonies in America would be expected to fight in that war. Quakers didn't believe in fighting in wars, but if Pennsylvania refused to help, the colony might be taken away from Penn.

It was soon apparent that Penn would have to return to England to defend himself. The family sailed for England in November 1701.

The situation was even worse than he had imagined when he reached London, and many of the problems weren't related to the war. His agent Philip Ford died soon after Penn's return, but Ford's family was demanding money that they said Penn owed Ford. Penn was disturbed to find that the man he had trusted with his accounts for years had been cheating him.

The money just wasn't there to pay off Ford's family, even if Penn really did owe it. Rents from his properties weren't being paid, and ships of goods his manager in Pennsylvania sent him to sell couldn't get through because of the war with the French. Hannah and John went to live with her family, and Letitia married.

A second son was born to the Penns, and then a daughter less than a year later. Hannah and the children remained with her parents in Bristol, while Penn tried to manage a multitude of political, financial, and colonial problems.

He began negotiations to sell Pennsylvania to the Crown and make it a royal colony. He didn't want to settle his debts in this manner but saw no other way to provide for his growing family.

Penn had sent William to Pennsylvania to handle colony affairs but called him home. A political opponent in Pennsylvania, David Lloyd, sent Penn a forthright letter about his son: "I supposed you will have a more ample account by others of the condition this poor Province is brought to by the late revels and disorders which young William Penn and his gang of loose fellows he accompanies with are found in, to the great grief of Friends and others in this place."[1]

Before any sale of the colony could take place, Penn was sent to the famous Fleet Prison in London—a debtor's prison. In those days a man could be sent to prison if he couldn't pay his debts.

Life was looking pretty grim for Penn, but his Quaker friends came to his rescue. They searched his financial records and discovered how much Ford had cheated him. The Ford family was strongly urged to accept less than the 16,000 pounds they said Penn owed them. At last they agreed to accept 7,600 pounds, which was paid mostly by nine Quakers, who took out mortgages on the Pennsylvania property.

Finally Penn could be reunited with his family, which now included five small children. The Penns moved to a large country home in Berkshire, England. There Penn remained, keeping busy with correspondence about Pennsylvania and the business of the Society of Friends. He continued to negotiate with the Crown about buying Pennsylvania.

At last a preliminary agreement was reached for the sale of the colony, but before it could be finalized, Penn suffered a stroke in 1712. He was never the same, although he lived for six more years. He was able to see visitors and go to the Quaker meetings in nearby Reading, but his speech and understanding had been affected. Hannah cared for him and took over administrative details for Pennsylvania. After a long decline, he died peacefully on July 30, 1718.

William Penn reflected well on the Quaker faith he pursued in his life. He was tolerant of differing views both political and religious but clung steadfastly to the values he learned from his Quaker teachers. He lived in America only four years during his two stays, but his influence was far broader than might be expected from such a brief time. He pioneered cooperation rather than conflict with the Native Americans, and he gave the settlers in his colony the right to rule themselves. He helped make Pennsylvania a refuge and home for people seeking a new life in a new land.

Penn didn't want Pennsylvania to be named after him and his family, but it is fitting that it is. William Penn was the heart of Pennsylvania then, and his influence extends to modern times.

For Your Information

Pennsbury Manor

William Penn's deputy in Pennsylvania, William Markham, negotiated with the Lenape and purchased the land for Penn's grand country home the summer before Penn arrived in America. He chose a spot on the Delaware about twenty-four miles from Philadelphia. The house would perch on a hill over the river.

The Lenape were paid with some money and also with wampum, which are long strings of beads, and kettles, guns, coats, hoes, and many other household items.

The house was carefully planned by Penn and reflected his love of nature and his desire to present his wife, Guli, with a perfect home. It was three stories, built of redbrick and surrounded by gardens and orchards. The rooms were large with casement windows that revealed a view of the countryside. In the custom of that time, there were many outbuildings, including a kitchen, washhouse, bake house, brew house, and stables.

Penn's beloved wife Guli never lived in Pennsbury, but his second wife and two of his children did live there when Penn returned to Pennsylvania.

It was a graciously furnished home, where Penn could entertain many visitors, who arrived via the river. The hot, humid summers and sharply cold winters were very different from what the Penns were used to in England, but the weather never dampened Penn's enthusiasm for Pennsbury Manor.

After Penn's death, the house and property were kept for several decades by his heirs. The estate was eventually sold and fell into ruin, after which it was sold many more times. Finally, in 1932, the ten acres of land where the house had stood were given to the state of Pennsylvania. Pennsbury Manor was carefully reconstructed and became open to the public.

Chapter Notes

Chapter 1 The New Colony

1. Samuel Janney, *The Life of William Penn; With Selections From His Correspondence and Autobiography* (Freeport, NY: Books for Libraries Press, 1970), pp. 194–95.

Chapter 3 The Inner Light

1. Samuel Pepys, *The Shorter Pepys* (Berkeley, Los Angeles: University of California Press, 1985), p. 130.
2. Samuel Janney, *The Life of William Penn; With Selections From His Correspondence and Autobiography* (Freeport, NY: Books for Libraries Press, 1970), p. 23.
3. Catherine Owens Peare, *William Penn* (Ann Arbor, MI: The University of Michigan Press, 1956), p. 56.

Chapter 4 The Holy Experiment

1. William Penn, *The Papers of William Penn, Volume Two, 1680–1684* (Philadelphia: University of Pennsylvania Press, 1982), p. 128.
2. Ibid., p. 270.
3. Ibid., p. 448.
4. Catherine Owens Peare, *William Penn* (Ann Arbor, MI: The University of Michigan Press, 1956), p. 70.

Chapter 5 Years of Struggle

1. Catherine Owens Peare, *William Penn* (Ann Arbor, MI: The University of Michigan Press, 1956), pp. 393–94.

Chronology

1644	Born on October 14 in London
1656	Penn family moves to Macroom Castle in Ireland
1660	After death of Cromwell, they move back to England; William Penn enrolls at Oxford
1662	Expelled from Oxford; father sends him to France
1665	Enters Lincoln's Inn to study law; the bubonic plague spreads through London
1666	Goes to Ireland to manage father's estates
1667	Returns to England a Quaker; is arrested; father disowns him for a while
1668	Imprisoned in the Tower of London, where he writes Quaker pamphlets
1670	Trial brings about new legal ruling that juries may not be punished for their verdicts
1672	Marries Gulielma Springett
1676	Arbitrates boundaries for West New Jersey
1681	Receives charter for Pennsylvania
1682	Arrives in Pennsylvania
1684	Returns to England to settle boundary dispute
1690	Arrested for treason but is cleared the following year
1694	Gulielma dies
1696	Marries Hannah Callowhill; son Springett dies
1699	Returns to Pennsylvania with Hannah and daughter Letitia
1701	Helps adopt new Frame of Government before returning to England
1703	Begins negotiations to sell Pennsylvania to the Crown
1708	Imprisoned for debts and then released
1712	Suffers first stroke
1718	Dies on July 30 at his home in Ruscombe, England

Timeline in History

1592	Shakespeare writes his first play, *Henry VI.*
1594	Ruins of Pompeii are discovered.
1607	Jamestown is founded.
1608	Refracting telescope is invented.
1611	King James translation of the Bible is published.
1620	*Mayflower* sails.
1632	Construction begins on the Taj Mahal.
1635	Postal service begins in Britain.
1643	Louis XIV becomes King of France at age five.
1653	Oliver Cromwell becomes Lord Protector of England.
1658	First advertisement for tea appears in England.
1660	Charles II is restored as King of England.
1661	Virginia legalizes slavery.
1665	Bubonic plague strikes London, killing up to 100,000 people.
1666	Great fire destroys much of London.
1673	Louis Joliet and Jacques Marquette explore Mississippi River.
1685	Composer Johann Sebastian Bach is born.
1692	In Massachusetts, the Salem witch trials begin.
1702	Queen Anne's War begins.
1714	First typewriter is patented in England.
1718	French found New Orleans.
1732	George Washington is born.
1738	Bottle opener is invented.
1739	John Wesley founds Methodist Church.
1742	Anders Celsius devises the centigrade thermometer.
1752	Benjamin Franklin demonstrates electricity with a kite and a key.

Further Reading

For Young Adults

Fradin, Dennis. *The Pennsylvania Colony.* Chicago: Children's Press, 1988.

Lutz, Norma Jean. *William Penn: Founder of Democracy.* Philadelphia: Chelsea House Publishers, 2000.

Robson, Pam. *All About the Great Plague.* Hove, England: Wayland, 2003.

Wilker, Josh. *The Lenape Indians.* Philadelphia: Chelsea House Publishers, 1994.

Works Consulted

Buranelli, Vincent. *The King and the Quaker; a Study of William Penn and James II.* Philadelphia: University of Pennsylvania Press, 1962.

Endy, Marvin, Jr. *William Penn and Early Quakerism.* Princeton, NJ: Princeton University Press, 1973.

Foster, Genevieve. *The World of William Penn.* New York: Charles Scribner's Sons, 1973.

Geiter, Mary. *William Penn.* Harlow, England: Pearson Education Limited, 2000.

Gray, Elizabeth Janet. *Penn.* New York: The Viking Press, 1938.

Hamm, Thomas. *The Quakers in America.* New York: Columbia University Press, 2003.

Janney, Samuel. *The Life of William Penn; With Selections From His Correspondence and Autobiography.* Freeport, NY: Books for Libraries Press, 1970.

Peare, Catherine Owens. *William Penn.* Ann Arbor, MI: The University of Michigan Press, 1956.

Penn, William. *The Papers of William Penn,* Volume Two, 1680–1684. Philadelphia: University of Pennsylvania Press, 1982.

——. *The Select Works of William Penn,* Volume One. New York: Kraus Reprint Co., 1971.

——. *The Select Works of William Penn,* Volume Three. New York: Kraus Reprint Co., 1971.

——. *Some Fruits of Solitude; Wise Sayings on the Conduct of Human Life.* Scottdale, PA: Herald Press, 2003.

——. *William Penn's Own Account of the Lenni Lenape or Delaware Indians.* Wilmington, DE: Mid-Atlantic Press, 1981.

Pepys, Samuel. *The Shorter Pepys.* Berkeley, Los Angeles: University of California Press, 1985.

William Penn and the Founding of Pennsylvania 1680–1684; a Documentary History. Edited by Jean Soderlund. Philadelphia: University of Pennsylvania Press, 1983.

On the Internet

Pennsbury Manor
http://www.pennsburymanor.org

William Penn; Visionary Proprietor
http://xroads.virginia.edu/~CAP/PENN/pnhome.html

Powell, Jim. "William Penn, America's First Great Champion for Liberty and Peace"
http://www.quaker.org/wmpenn.html

"Excerpts from 'Frame of Government of Pennsylvania' by William Penn, 1682"
http://www.constitution.org/bcp/frampenn.htm

The Cromwell Association
http://www.olivercromwell.org/

Glossary

allegiance (ah-LEE-jins)
Loyalty to a person or cause.

arbitrate (AR-bih-trayt)
To help settle a dispute.

gout (GOWT)
Inflammation of the joints caused by crystal deposits from the blood.

heresy (HEH-rah-see)
Religious ideas that go against the ideas of a dominant church.

latitude (LAA-tih-tood)
The distance between the equator and a point north or south on the earth's surface measured in degrees.

mortgage (MOR-gij)
A loan on property.

nonconformist (non-kun-FOR-mist)
A person who acts in a way that doesn't agree with a generally accepted rule or practice.

politician (pah-lih-TIH-shen)
A person who is involved in party politics as it relates to running a government.

pound (POWND)
A unit of money used in Britain.

proprietor (pro-PRY-eh-tor)
Someone who has a legal title or exclusive right to some property.

quitrent (KWIT-rent)
A type of land tax.

rituals (RIH-choo-ells)
A set of actions always done in the same way.

toleration (tah-ler-AY-shun)
The act of accepting or respecting differences in others, including differences in race, opinions, and beliefs.

Index

Amyraut, Moïse 22
Baltimore, Lord 9, 33, 34, 37
bubonic plague 23, 27
Carrickfergus 24, 25
Charles I 13, 14, 19
Charles II 7, 8, 14, 18, 21, 23, 25, 31, 37
Coaquannock 9
Cromwell, Oliver 13, 14, 15–17, 18, 19, 21, 35
Duke of York 23, 30, 37
(*see also* James II)
Endeavour 28, 34
Ford, Philip 39, 40
Fox, George 30, 35
Frame of Government 32, 33
Great Treaty 10
Holy Experiment 32
James II 37–38
Lenni Lenape 9, 10, 11, 33–34, 42
Lincoln's Inn 22, 23, 24
Lloyd, David 40
Loe, Thomas 16–17, 24
Louis XIV 22
Macroom Castle 16–17, 23, 24
Markham, William 9, 42
Mary, Queen 37–38
Native Americans 8, 9, 32, 33
(*see also* Lenni Lenape)
Parliament 13, 14, 19, 31, 37
Penn, Gulielma Springett 30, 32, 34, 38, 42
Penn, Hannah Callowhill 36, 38, 39, 40, 41, 42
Penn, John (son) 39, 40
Penn, Letitia (daughter) 30, 39, 40
Penn, Margaret (mother) 14, 15, 22
Penn, Margaret (sister) 15, 24
Penn, Richard (brother) 16
Penn, Springett (son) 30, 38
Penn, Sir William (father) 12, 13, 14–16, 17–18, 21, 22–26, 30, 31
Penn, William
- arrested 25, 26, 29, 38, 40
- birth of 13
- called Onas 10
- death of 41
- education of 15, 21–22, 23
- expelled from Oxford 22
- first site for Philadelphia 9
- in Fleet Debtor Prison 40
- granted Pennsylvania Charter 8, 31
- in Ireland 16–17, 18, 23–25, 26
- marries Gulielma Springett 30
- marries Hannah Callowhill 38
- meets Native Americans at Shackamaxon 10
- at New Castle, 1682 7, 34
- in Pennsylvania, 1682 7, 32, 39
- returns to England, 1684 34
- suffers stroke 41
- visits Paris 22

Penn, William III (son) 30, 39, 40
Pennsbury Manor 9, 32, 42
Pepys, Samuel 20, 21
Philadelphia 9, 10, 32, 39
Puritans 15, 21, 22
Quakers 16, 22, 23, 24, 25, 30, 31, 35, 38, 39, 40, 41
Tower of London 13, 16, 18, 26
Treaty Elm 6, 10